THE ULTIMATE WOOD PELLET GRILL AND SMOKER COOKBOOK

COMPLETE SMOKER COOKBOOK FOR SMOKING AND GRILLING, THE MOST DELICIOUS AND MOUTHWATERING PELLET GRILLING BBQ RECIPES FOR YOUR WHOLE FAMILY

CONTENTS

Foreword

BBQ is not just a method of cooking food– it's an experience. It's a culture, a link to our past, a tribute to the resourcefulness of our earliest forbearers, and a reminder of times both great and terrible.

It's about the age-old mainstays of good food, good friends, and good times. It's rugged but romantic.

It's smoke and chatter.

As the food cooks, the aromas become as enticing as the spectacle itself. It becomes not just a conversation piece, but a conversation starter.

Here are some of my most popular dishes, tips, and techniques that I've learned over nearly four-decades of cooking in, over, and with fire and smoke.

If you're looking for great recipes and insights for taking your BBQ and grill skills to the next level, you've come to the right place.

Welcome to the fire!

What is BBQ?

First and foremost, we have to answer the question, "What is BBQ?"
The word barbecue, when used as a noun, can refer to the cooking method, the meat cooked in this way, or to an event where this style of food is featured.

Used as an adjective, "barbecued" refers to foods cooked by this method. The term is also used as a verb for the act of cooking food in this manner. Barbecuing is usually done out-of-doors by smoking the meat over wood or charcoal. Restaurant barbecue may be cooked in large brick or metal ovens designed for that purpose.

There are numerous regional variations of barbecuing, and it is practiced in many areas of the world, we'll take a look at those a bit later.

NOTE: Despite popular marketing, the cooking apparatus used to cook with is not a "barbeque", it is either a GRILL, a SMOKER, or some modification, or combination of the two.

Barbecues today have taken on new meaning yet again with the emergence of competitive barbecue.

Competitive barbecue competitions are held throughout the country in which people will compete by cooking barbecue and having it judged by the events judges. The constraints of what one may barbecue and the qualities that are judged vary by competition.

Usually competitions are held in large open areas, where spectators are being admitted as well, and barbecue is served to all.

A Bit of History

The English word Barbecue and cognates in other languages come from the Spanish word barbacoa. Etymologists believe this to be derived from barabicu found in the language of the Arawak people of the Caribbean and the Timucua of Florida.

The Oxford English Dictionary traces the word to Haiti and translates it as a "framework of sticks set upon posts".

Gonzalo Fernández De Oviedo y Valdés, a Spanish explorer, was the first to use the word "barbecoa" in 1526 "Diccionario de la Lengua Española" of the Real Academia Española.

After Columbus landed in the Americas in 1492, the Spaniards apparently found native Haitians slowly roasting meat over a grill consisting of a wooden framework resting on sticks above a fire.

The flames and smoke rose and enveloped the meat, giving it a unique flavor. The same framework was also used as protection from nocturnal animal attacks.

Traditional barbacoa involved digging a hole in the ground and placing some meat—usually a whole lamb—above a pot so the juices can be used to make a broth. It is then covered with leaves and coals, and set alight. The cooking process takes a few hours. Olaudah Equiano, an African abolitionist, described this method of roasting alligators among the Mosquito People (Miskito people) on his journeys to Cabo Gracias a Dios.

Linguists have suggested the word barbacoa migrated from the Caribbean and into other languages and cultures; it moved from Caribbean dialects into Spanish, then Portuguese, French, and English. According to the OED, the first recorded use of the word in English was a verb in 1661, in Edmund Hickeringill's Jamaica Viewed.

The word barbecue was published in English in 1672 as a verb from the writings of John Lederer, following his travels in the North American southeast in 1669-70. The first known use of the word as a noun was in 1697 by the British buccaneer William Dampier.

In his New Voyage Round the World, Dampier wrote, " … and the meat lay there all night, upon our Borbecu's, or frames of Sticks, raised about 3 foot from the Ground".

Pellet Grills & Smokers

Pellet smokers use pellet bio-mass fuel made from recycled hardwood sawdust, which is formed into clean burning wood pellets.

By reducing pure hardwood to sawdust, and then compressing it into uniform, food-grade pellets, these smokers make it possible to deliver precise amounts of hardwood pellets from the hopper, to the burner.

Be sure that you are using only food-grade pellets for cooking with your pellet smoker, never "heating pellets."

Many types of heating pellets are made from woods that you wouldn't want to use for smoking, like pine or spruce.

These woods will ruin the flavor of your food.

Heating pellets may also be made from wood products like plywood or particle board, and include binding agents that could also sour the flavor of your meat, or even be poisonous.

In appearance, most pellet grills & smokers look similar to the classic offset barrel smoker, with a side-mounted hopper replacing the firebox.

An electric-powered auger feeds a measured amount of pellets, at a specific speed, into a burner, while an electric powered fan keeps them smoldering.

Pellet smokers pre-heat quickly, create minimal ash, and allow you to "start it and forget it" (to an extent), instead of constantly needing to feed and maintain fire and smoke.

In other words, you can "low & slow" BBQ overnight, without losing your beauty sleep!

Wood Pellet Grills are a great way to combine the best aspects of both grilling and BBQ, while achieving the unique flavors and textures of each!

Know Your Smoker

Knowing which wood to use when smoking meats, is often the most confusing part of the process for those new to BBQ. There are a lot of choices, and even more There are so many choices and variations. How do you know where to start? I've probably tested just about every combination out there, and I tend to agree with these common suggestions:

Applewood Apple smoke has a light, fruity, flavor that imparts a slightly sweetness to the meat. Apple is great with fish, chicken, and pork ribs.

Cherry: Cherry smoke is a little stronger than apple, but still considered a mild smoke. It's best for smoking cheese and poultry.

Alder: Moderately mild and still slightly sweet, alder smoke is my go to for fish (especially salmon) and seafood. My native American ancestors of the Pacific coast used alder to smoke salmon and steelhead for thousands of years, Test it with chicken and pork, too.

Oa: Ah, oak...the universal smoke! Oak smoke compliments just about anything, but it's the standard for most pros, when smoking pork. Often, especially in the South, is' blended with pecan, as well.

Mesquite: I don't use mesquite often, as it can often overpower the flavor of most domesticated meats. However, it's perfect for stronger (some use the term "gamey") meats like venison, buffalo, and other wild game meats. Finally, remember...it's a process.

Keep experimenting with as many combinations of meat and smoke you can lay your hands on. Build up a catalog in your head (or better, keep a journal), of the various flavor profiles you create.

Practice this enough h, and you reach a point where you just...know...what smoke would best compliment it.

For more tips on matching meats to smoke, see our Wood Smoking Chart at the end of this book.

Beef & Lamb

Soy-Honey Flank Steak

Serves: 6, **Prep Time:** 8 Hours, Cook **Time:** 15 Minutes

Ingredients
- ½ C red wine vinegar
- ¼ C soy sauce
- ¼ C minced fresh ginger
- 3 Tbsp. honey
- 1 Tbsp. salad oil
- 1 tsp black pepper
- 4 cloves garlic, pressed
- 2 lbs. flank steak
- Lime wedges (optional)

Directions
1. In a gallon-size resealable bag, mix together vinegar, soy sauce, ginger, honey, oil, garlic, and pepper. Add steak (close bag) and turn to coat. Refrigerate 6-8 hours, turning several times. Let rest at room temperature for 30 minutes.
2. Drain steak; discard marinade. Lightly oil pellet grill and bring to high heat.
3. Lay steak on the pre-heated grate and sear, turning to brown evenly, until pink in the thickest part for medium-rare (125°F), 5 - 6 minutes per side.
4. Transfer steak to a cutting board and allow to rest 5 minutes. Thinly slice meat across the grain to serve. Offer lime wedges to squeeze over individual portions to taste.

Rare - 120°F Medium Rare - 125°F Medium - 130°F

Flat Iron Chili Steaks

Serves: 6 **Prep Time:** 15 Minutes Cook **Time:** 15 Minutes

Ingredients
- 2 flat iron steaks, 1lbs. each
- 3 Tbsp. olive oil
- 2 Tbsp. onion, minced
- 3 cloves garlic, minced
- 1 Tbsp. balsamic vinegar
- 2 ½ tsp chili powder
- 1 tsp hickory salt
- 1 tsp smoked paprika
- 1/4 teaspoon black pepper

Directions
1. Season steaks with hickory salt and place is a gallon-size resealable bag.

2. Combine marinade ingredients and pour over steak, turn to coat, and seal up the bag. Let stand at room temp for 10 minutes.

3. Preheat pellet grill for medium high heat. Remove steak from dish, reserving marinade.

4. Place meat on grill and allow to cook for 13-15 minutes. Brush often with reserved marinade during cooking process.

5. When meat reaches desired "doneness," remove from heat and allow it to rest for a five minutes before slicing.

Perfect Steaks

Serves: 6, **Prep Time:** 1 Hour, Cook **Time:** 20 Minutes

To grill the perfect steak, you get what you pay for. Go with t-bone, rib-eye or NY strips. If you can find a butcher that ages their beef 30 days, you'll taste the difference.

Ingredients
- 3lbs. NY Strip Steaks 2" thick.
- Coarse sea salt
- Fresh ground black pepper

Steak Butter:
- Remove steaks from refrigerator 1 hour before cooking, pat dry and allow to rest at room temp. Oil your pellet grill grate and heat to highest temp. I like to use a mix of oak and pecan pellets for steaks.
- If you can hold your hand six inches above the grill and count to two, it's not hot enough!
- ½ stick of sweet cream butter
- 1 Tbsp. lemon juice
- ¼ cup chopped Italian parsley
- 2 Tbsp. minced garlic
- 1 Tbsp. Worcestershire sauce
- dash red pepper flakes

Directions
1. Melt butter, stirring to combine ingredients (set aside two tsp of parsley for garnish) and pour into a baking pan.
2. Cooking: place steaks on grill and cook until lightly charred (about two minutes.) Don't move steaks until the first side is finished cooking, then use tongs to turn. Flip steaks to second side and grill 2 more minutes.

3. Remove from the grill and place in baking pan, dredging both sides in the steak butter.

4. Return steaks to grill, sprinkle each side with sea salt and pepper, and finish cooking – you're looking for an internal temp of 115f. Once steaks reach that (2-3 additional minutes per side) move them back to the baking pan, dredge in butter again, and allow to rest 10-15 minutes at room temp.

5. To serve, drizzle a little of the butter and juice mixture (from the pan) onto your cutting board and slice steaks thinly across the grain. Pour a little of the butter/juice onto a plate, top with a fan of steak slices, and spoon a bit more butter over the top.

6. Sprinkle with remaining chopped parsley and serve immediately.

"Da Best" Burgers

Serves: 3 **Prep Time:** 1 ½ Hours Cook **Time:** 10 Minutes

Fletcher Davis of Athens, Texas, is believed to have sold hamburgers at his café in the late 1880s, then brought them to the 1904 St. Louis World's Fair. The McDonald's hamburger chain claims the inventor was an unknown food vendor at that same World's Fair. The hamburger bun was invented in 1916 by a fry cook named Walter Anderson, who later co-founded White Castle in 1921.

Ingredients
- 3 Tbsp. lemon pepper
- 1 Tbsp. ground thyme
- 1 Tbsp. paprika
- 1 tsp granular garlic
- ½ tsp sugar
- ½ tsp seasoned salt
- ½ tsp fresh black pepper
- pinch cayenne pepper
- 1lbs. ground beef, 20% fat

Directions
1. Mix spices, except for salt, with ground beef about an hour before cooking, to allow flavors to marry.
2. Form 3 - ½ inch thick patties, slightly larger than the buns, and sprinkle with salt just before grilling. Preheat one side of pellet grill to high.
3. Sear your patties on each side over a high heat until a crust forms. This should take about one to one-and-a-half minutes.
4. Move patties to the "cool" side of the pellet grill and cook another ten minutes, flipping once.

Fritas

(Cuban Hamburgers)

Serves: 6 **Prep Time:** 2 ½ Hours Cook **Time:** 10 Minutes

Ingredients
- 1 lbs. ground beef
- ½ lbs. Cuban chorizo
- ½ lbs. ground pork
- 1/4 C milk
- ¼ C bread crumbs
- 1/3 tsp paprika
- 3 Tbsp. minced onion
- 1 egg
- 2 tsp sal
- 1 tsp Worcester sauce
- ½ tsp black pepper
- Six soft white rolls, split
- 12oz curly fries, cooked

Directions
1. Combine all the ground meat and chorizos. Soak bread crumbs in milk, beat eggs and add to the milk together with all the remaining ingredients.
2. Add to the meat mixture and mix well using the hands. Shape into six patties. Place them in the fridge for a couple of hours, before grilling directly over high heat.
3. Serve on toasted rolls topped with crisp-cooked shoestring fries.

There is a big difference between Cuban chorizo and Mexican chorizo. Mexican chorizo has a grainier texture and tends to fall apart when you split the casing where as Cuban chorizo has more of a solid sausage texture. Also, Cuban chorizo has no hot peppers, and is packed with lots of fresh cilantro.

Smokey Tri-Tip

Serves: 12-18. **Prep Time:** 12 hours Cook **Time:** 40 minutes

Ingredients
- 2 (4-pound) tri-tips, trimmed
- 1 cup lemon juice
- 1 cup soybean oil
- ½ cup white sugar
- ½ cup soy sauce
- ½ cup black pepper
- ½ cup garlic powder
- ¼ cup seasoned salt
- ½ cup chopped fresh garlic
- ½ cup chopped dried onions

Directions
1. To make the marinade, mix all of the ingredients except for the beef in a large mixing bowl. Combine marinade and meat in a vacuum marinade tumbler and process, per the machine's Directions.
2. If you don't have a vacuum marinade tumbler, place the trimmed tri-tips in a plastic container and pour the marinade over. Let stand in the refrigerator for at least 12 hours (24 is better.)
3. Heat pellet grill to medium temperature, using oak pellets to smoke. Place tri-tips on grill at a 45 degree angle to establish grill marks and cook about 35 minutes, or until cooked to desired "doneness."
4. Remove the tri-tips from the grill and let rest about 2 to 5 minutes before slicing.
5. Serve on steamed stadium rolls, or over sticky Jasmine rice as bento, with your favorite sauce. I like a sweet chili sauce.

Mock Tri-Tip

Serves: 12-18 **Prep Time:** 12 hours Cook **Time:** 1 hour 30 minutes
Use an herb/spice butter to help add moisture, and an instant-read thermometer,
so you don't have to cut into meat to check for doneness, allowing valuable juices
to escape.

Ingredients
- 2 - 4 lbs. chuck roast
- 1 Tbsp. garlic powder
- 1 Tbsp. onion powder
- 1 Tbsp. celery salt
- 1 tsp oregano Italian dressing

Steak butter
- 1 lbs. sweet cream butter
- 4 Tbsp. seasoned salt
- 2 Tbsp. garlic powder
- 2 Tbsp. smoked paprika
- 1 Tbsp. coarse black pepper

Directions
1. Marinade meat overnight in oil and vinegar based Italian dressing, remove
   from marinade, and blot dry.

2. Mix all spices and rub both sides of roasts, then let stand at room
   temperature for 1 hour. Warm butter and add seasoned salt, garlic, paprika,
   and pepper, blending well. Cool slightly until spreadable. Heat one side of
   your pellet grill to high, and the other to low, and lightly oil the cooking grate.
   Place meat on hot side of the grill, fat side up, and grill five minutes per side.

3. Move steaks to "cooler" side of the grill and turn off the hot side.

4. You can place a drip pan under it to catch the drips which will make a great gravy later.

5. With the pellet grill on low cook for about 1 hour or until it reaches your desired doneness. Remove roasts from grill, flip, smear with remaining steak-butter, and allow to rest 15 minutes to before cutting in 1/8 " slices across the grain.

Teriyaki Tri-tip Sliders

Serves: 32 Sliders **Prep Time:** 24 Hours Cook **Time:** 30 Minutes

Ingredients
- 4 beef tri-tips (2 lb./ea.)
- 2 tsp dry mustard
- 4 C soy sauce
- 1 C brown sugar
- 3 C thinly sliced onion
- 2 C sake
- 2 C mirin
- 4 Tbsp. minced garlic
- 4 Tbsp. thinly sliced fresh ginger
- 2 tsp pepper

Directions
1. Pour soy sauce, sugar, onion, sake, mirin, garlic, ginger, pepper, and mustard into 4 – 1 gallon-size resealable bags. Add one tri-tip to each bag, and seal. Chill 24 hours, turning occasionally.

2. Lay tri-tips on a lightly oiled pellet grill over pre-heated to high heat, turning every 5 minutes, until 125° to 130° on an instant read thermometer, or about 25 minutes.

3. Transfer tri-tip to a cutting board. Let rest about 5 minutes, and then cut across the grain into thin, slanting slices. Place 1-2 slices on a split potato roll, top with Simple Tangy Coleslaw, or pickled ginger, and serve.

True Texas Brisket

Serves: 45-60 **Prep Time:** 13 Hours Cook **Time:** 14 Hours

Ingredients
- 3 whole brisket, 12-14 lbs.
- 6 C Renner's Amazing Brisket Rub
- 2 C Mustard glaze (see below)
- 6 C Oak wood pellets

Directions
1. The night before you plan to begin cooking, rinse the briskets, and pat dry. Place the briskets in large disposable pans and generously apply Renner
2. 's Amazing Brisket Rub (pg. 116) to all meat surfaces. Refrigerate overnight.
3. Remove the brisket from refrigerator 1 hour prior to smoking and let stand at room temperature.
4. Mop the entire brisket with Mustard Sauce, then sprinkle with another light coat of black pepper. Place brisket fat side up in a smoker at a preheated temperature of 200 to 225 degrees F. Smoke 6 hours. Place brisket on 2 pieces of heavy-duty foil and seal tightly.
5. Continue to cook in smoker (or oven) another 4 to 6 hours, or until internal temperature reaches 190 degrees F. Move brisket, still wrapped in foil, to a cooler, and rest 2 hours.

Remove brisket from foil and let stand 30 minutes. Slice brisket against the grain into ¼ inch thickness.

Mustard Glaze
- 1 cup yellow mustard
- 1 teaspoon ground black pepper
- 1 teaspoon sea salt

Mix all ingredients in a medium saucepan. Reduce heat to low and simmer for 10 minutes.

Brisket Tips

Preparing: If you have a frozen brisket, let it thaw in the refrigerator for 2 days to defrost thoroughly. One hour before you plan to begin cooking, take the brisket from the refrigerator.

Remove the plastic packaging, rinse brisket well with cool water, and pat dry. DO NOT remove the fat; that will provide moisture and flavor as the brisket cooks.

Reheating: Spritz the meat with apple juice and add 1/8" of the same juice to the bottom of the pan.

Cover tightly with foil and heat in a 200-250°F oven until warmed to your liking. Just before serving, brush on a thin layer of your favorite barbecue sauce to give the slices a nice sheen.

If you prefer to keep the cooked brisket whole and unsliced, wrap it in foil and refrigerate. Before reheating, open the foil and add some juice or broth as described above, and close the foil tightly.

Heat in the oven or smoker at 200-250°F until warmed to your liking, then slice and serve.

Resting Time: At a minimum, place the brisket on a rimmed baking pan, cover loosely with foil, and let rest 30 minutes before slicing. 60-90 minutes is better.

Brisket Yield: When you take into account the trimming of the brisket before and after cooking, plus the shrinkage that occurs during cooking, don't be surprised if you end up with a 50% yield of edible meat from a whole, untrimmed brisket.

That means 6 pounds of edible meat from a 12 pound brisket.

Depending on the brisket and the internal temp you cook it to, it may be as low as 40% or as high as 60%.

If you're cooking brisket for a party, figure 4-5 ounces of meat per sandwich or 6 ounces of sliced meat on a plate (8 ounces for hearty eaters). Using a 40% yield, just to be safe, a 12 pound brisket yields 19 4-ounce sandwiches or almost 13 6-ounce plate servings.

Burnt Ends: Traditionally, burnt ends sold in restaurants were the dry edges and leftover bits and pieces of the brisket flat after slicing, mixed with barbecue sauce. These morsels were highly prized for their intense, smoky flavor.

Today, famous barbecue joints like Arthur Bryant's in Kansas City can't meet the demand for burnt ends using leftover bits, so they make a facsimile by cubing fully cooked brisket flats, placing the cubes in a pan and smoking them for a couple of hours, then adding sauce and smoking for a couple more hours.

Another approach for making burnt ends is to separate the point section from the flat section after the flat is done, then return the point to the cooker for smoke for an additional 4-6 hours.

Chop the point, mix with barbecue sauce, and enjoy!

Smokey Beef Ribs

Serves: 10 **Prep Time:** 12 Hours Cook **Time:** 2 Hours

Ingredients
- 6 full beef rib racks, trimmed
- 1 C Beef Rib Rub (pg. 117)
- 3 C Beef Rib Mop (pg. 124)
- 3 C favorite BBQ sauce
- 2 cans of beer

Directions
1. The night before cooking, rub beef ribs and wrap in plastic. Refrigerate 12-18 hours.

2. Place disposable pan, with beer, beneath the grill rack to catch drips and prevent flare-ups. Allow ribs to come to room temp, and Preheat your pellet grill and prepare for indirect grilling.

3. Place ribs on the hot side of grill, searing for 2-3 minutes on each side. Then move to "cool side" to cook indirectly.

4. Grill for 1 to 1 1/2 hours turning and mopping every 15 minutes.

5. Remove ribs from grill and rest, tented loosely in foil, for 30 minutes.

6. Serve with your favorite BBQ sauce (warmed) on the side.

Mexican Barbacoa

Serves: 12 **Prep Time:** 20 Minutes Cook **Time:** 12 Hours

Ingredients
- 3 Lbs. Beef chuck roast
- 1 Qt cold Water
- 2 - Chiles Ancho
- 5 Cloves garlic
- 1 Large onion, quartered
- 2 banana leaves
- 2 Tamarind pods
- 2 Lg bay leaves
- 1 tsp cumin
- 3 Tbsp. Fresh cilantro, chopped
- Mexican sour cream

Directions
1. Preheat pellet grill to high using hickory pellets. Sear meat 10 minutes per-side until starting to char. Turn one side of grill off and reduce heat of second side to medium.
2. Move the roast to the "off" side and barbeque, with indirect heat, for one hour, adding smoke every 15 minutes.
3. Drape 2 banana leaves over a "deep-dish" disposable pan, pressing to the bottom, then add a layer of chopped onion.
4. Remove roast from grill and place in the pan on top of the onion, then add the cold water, chiles ancho, tamarind, bay leaves and garlic, fold banana leaves over the top and secure with a couple of toothpicks.
5. Place pan, uncovered, in a pre-heated oven (425d) for 20 minutes.

6. Once simmering, reduce heat to 175d and cover the pan with foil. Let simmer ten hours, turning the meat 2-3 times.

7. (You'll be "stirring" the last couple of times.)

8. After 10 hours, give the tamarind pod a few good smacks and pick off the shell, the stem and the thick fibers that run down its length. Remove the seeds and add the gummy pulp to the pan. Add the cumin and simmer one hour more.

9. Then, fish out the bones, ancho chiles, bay leaves, and banana leaves.

10. Pour off half of the fluids, and place the pan, uncovered, back in the oven for about an hour to let the juices bake down and thicken. Stir frequently.

11. Just before bringing to the table, stir in most of the chopped Cilantro, and quickly top with dollops of Mexican sour cream.

12. Serve with your favorite guacamole, salsa, and hot tortillas.

If you're a true chile-head, roast some whole jalapeños in the pellet grill, slice, core (to remove the seeds) and serve on the side.

Salt & Pepper Beef Tenderloin

Serves: 12 **Prep Time:** 90 Minutes Cook **Time:** 1 Hour

Ingredients
- 3 beef tenderloins, 4lbs. each
- 1 C fine sea salt
- 3/4 C olive oil
- 6 Tbsp. black pepper
- Crumbled blue cheese (garnish)

Directions
1. Buy the tenderloins pre-trimmed, around 5-6 lbs. each. Pre-cut 7-8 pieces of kitchen twine, each about 18" long, for each tenderloin.
2. Fold the tail end of the roast under the center section to create an even diameter and tie up each tenderloin evenly with 8 pieces of twine.
3. Trim any loose ends. Pat dry and sprinkle all sides with 1-1/2 tablespoons of salt.
4. Wrap in plastic wrap and let sit at room temperature for one hour. This step allows the salt to penetrate the meat and will help it cook more evenly.
5. Just before cooking, apply a thin coat of olive oil and sprinkle with a good amount of freshly cracked black pepper; sear over direct medium heat until well-marked, about 20 minutes, turning a quarter turn every 5 minutes.
6. Continue grilling over indirect medium heat until internal temperature reaches 135° for medium rare, 10-20 minutes.
7. Remove the tenderloin from the grill and let rest for 5-10 minutes. Serve whole or cut into ¾-1 inch slices.
8. Sprinkle with a little crumbled blue cheese and serve warm.

Thai Beef Satays

Serves: 16 **Prep Time:** 12 Hours Cook **Time:** 20 Minutes

Ingredients
- 2 lb. sirloin tips
- 60 bamboo skewers
- 2 Tbsp. red curry Paste
- 26 oz coconut milk
- 2 Tbsp. fish sauce
- 2 Tbsp. minced ginger

Directions
1. Cut sirloin into thin strips

2. In a medium saucepan, heat coconut milk with the curry paste. Stir until smooth and bubbling.

3. Turn off heat. Add fish sauce and minced ginger. Stir well and pour into shallow dish. Add the beef, making sure each piece is well coated.

4. Cover and refrigerate for six hours or overnight.

5. Soak bamboo skewers in cold water 2 hours before grilling to keep them from burning on grill.

6. Thread meat onto skewers and sear on a pre-heated pellet grill (high heat) for 3 minutes on each side or until done.

Castilian Roast Leg of Lamb

Serves: 20 **Prep Time:** 12 Hours Cook **Time:** 20 Minutes

Ingredients
- 2 - 6 lbs. legs of lamb (butterflied)
- 4 Tbsp. of olive oil
- Freshly ground black pepper
- Salt
- 2 tsp fresh thyme
- 4 cloves of garlic sliced
- 2 C of dry white wine
- 4 C of water
- 2 Tbsp. of wine vinegar
- Juice of 1 lemon

Directions
1. Rub the lamb with half of olive oil, season it with salt and pepper and rub the thyme over the surface of the lamb. Let the lamb sit for an hour to absorb the flavors.
2. Put the white wine, water, vinegar and lemon juice into a pan and bring to the boil. Allow to cool. Make some slits in the leg of lamb and put some slices of garlic into them, baste with ½ of the liquid, and then rub the lamb with the rest of the olive oil.
3. Heat the grill on high on all burners to start.
4. Place the lamb, fat side down, on the grill on the hot side. Sear one side for 4 minutes, then flip the lamb over to sear the other side for another 4 minutes.
5. Then move the roasts to the "cool" side of the grill and lower the heat to medium low.

1. You will want to maintain a temperature of 300-350°F. Baste again, and then cover the grill and let cook for an additional 35-45 minutes until a meat thermometer inserted into the thickest part of the roast registers 130°F (for medium rare).

2. Transfer to a cutting board with a well to catch the juices. Cover with foil and let rest for 10-15 minutes.

3. Cut across the grain, 1/4 to 1/2-inch thick slices. Serve slices on a warm platter; pour meat juices over the slices.

Moroccan Whole Roast Lamb

Serves: 30 **Prep Time:** 48 Hours Cook **Time:** 8 Hours

Ingredients
- 1 - Grass-fed, three-month-old lamb around 36-40 pounds, skinned. As much surface fat removed as possible.
- Chermoula
- 4 sweet onions, pureed
- 2 C fresh garlic, ground
- 2 C butter
- 2 C olive oil
- Salt to taste
- 3 bunches cilantro, diced
- ¼ C cumin
- ½ C coriander
- ½ C paprika
- 2 Tbsp. fresh black pepper

Directions
1. Combine all chermoula ingredients and mix together over medium heat until it forms a paste. (Chermoula is a Moroccan marinade.)
2. Allow chermoula to set overnight.
3. Rub this mixture over the surface of the lamb making sure to get it evenly distributed, inside and out. Plan on allowing the chermoula to sit on the meat for 48 hours before you cook.
4. Bring your pellet grill/smoker to 250F, and place the lamb in your pellet smoker, ribs side down. Connect the wired thermometer probe on the leg, be careful not to touch the bone.
5. Smoke 6-8 hours to an internal temperature of 145F

Fresh Lamb: Rare 140, Medium Rare 145, Medium 160

PORK

Pulled or Chopped?

At a Pig Picking', the barbecue is likely going to be pulled from the bone and served in chunks. This "pulled pork" barbecue is mighty hard to beat. Add a finishing sauce if you like.

The barbecue served in a restaurant is usually chopped, and addition of finishing sauce during chopping is common.

If you decide to go the chopped route, be sure to remember that chopped and pureed isn't the same! Properly cooked barbecue is very tender and slicing is a tricky business when it is warm. Allow the barbecue to cool somewhat for consistent success.

Plunk it between a soft bun of white bread or eat it plain.

Always cook pork shoulders with the fat-cap up, and marinate, wrapped in plastic wrap, 12-24 hours.

Be sure to cook pulled pork to an internal temperature of 195d and let rest 20-30 minutes before chopping.

Pork should be pulled while warm. My preference is to pull the pork after resting and mix in some extra rub before serving.

To reheat, spritz with apple juice or drippings, cover tightly with foil, and heat in a 200-250°F oven or smoker, stirring occasionally, until warmed to your liking.

Pierna Criolla

Serves: 18 **Prep Time:** 12 Hours Cook **Time:** 2.5 Hours

Ingredients
- 1 - 8 lbs. pork shoulder
- 8 slices bacon
- 1/2 lb. ham
- 1 bottle Malta
- 1 cup guava shells
- 1 cup Mojo (pg. 125)
- 1 cup prunes
- 4 Tbsp. Adobo Spices
- 2 cups brown sugar
- 2 Tbsp. sea salt

Directions
1. Debone and flatten meat so that it may be rolled.
2. If the pork shoulder is very fatty, a small amount may be removed.
3. Score fat well and marinate for a minimum of 12 hours in the Mojo, and Adobo.
4. Sear both sides of roast on a very hot grate until dark brown and charred in spots, using apple-wood pellets for a smoky flavor.
5. Remove roast to cutting board, and line unrolled roast with ham slices, bacon slices, prunes and guava shells. Roll meat carefully to keep the filling inside. Tie firmly with a butcher cord.
6. Cover with brown sugar and 1/2 bottle of Malta.
7. Cook for one hour in the pellet smoker at 325.
8. At this point, turn the meat, cover with the remaining Malta and cook for an extra hour, or until you reach a meat temperature of 180.

9. Allow to cool at least 30 minutes and cut into fine slices. Pour the drippings over the meat after slicing the meat.

 These ingredients can be found at most Hispanic grocery stores.

Sweet & Spicy Pork Kabobs

Serves: 6 **Prep Time:** 24 Hours Cook **Time:** 10 Minutes

Ingredients
- 2lbs. boneless pork, 1-inch cubes
- ¾ C olive oil
- 1 Tbsp. Worcestershire sauce
- 1 tsp dried thyme
- 2 tsp black pepper
- ½ tsp cayenne
- ¾ C cider vinegar
- ¼ C sugar
- 4 Tbsp. lemon juice
- 1 Tbsp. oregano
- 2 cloves garlic, minced
- 1 tsp salt

Directions
1. Mix together first 11 ingredients, place in sealable bag and refrigerate 24 hours; thread onto skewers.
2. Grill on high heat, basting with reserved marinade, for 4-5 minutes; turn and grill another 4-5 minutes.
3. Sprinkle with salt and serve.

Big Island Pork Kabobs

Serves: 6 **Prep Time:** 24 Hours Cook **Time:** 15 Minutes

Ingredients
- 3 lbs. Pork tenderloin
- 3 C margarita mix
- 3 clove garlic – minced
- 2 lg bell peppers
- 4 lbs. whole mushrooms
- ¼ C butter - softened
- 4 tsp lime juice
- 1 teaspoon sugar
- 3 Tbsp. minced parsley

Directions
1. For marinate: combine margarita mix and garlic.
2. Cut pork into 1-inch cubes, place in a sealable plastic bag; pour marinade over to cover. Marinate overnight.
3. Blend together the butter, lime juice, Splenda, and parsley; set aside.
4. Thread pork cubes onto skewers, alternating with mushrooms and pepper, cut into eighths.
5. Grill over high heat, basting with butter mixture, for 10-15 minutes, turning frequently.

If you're using bamboo skewers, soak them in water 20-30 minutes before using.

Asian Pork Sliders

Serves: 8 **Prep Time:** 24 Hours Cook **Time:** 15 Minutes

Ingredients
- 2 lbs. ground pork
- 1 C diced green onion
- 2 tsp garlic powder
- 2 Tbsp. soy sauce
- 2 tsp brown sugar
- 1 C shredded lettuce
- 1 tsp cornstarch
- Honey-mustard dressing
- 16 sesame rolls, split

Directions
1. Mix all ingredients (except soy sauce) and form 16 equal patties. Brush each patty with soy sauce, and grill over high heat, turning once.
2. Serve with honey mustard and cucumber spears.

I like to chill the seasoned meat and then spread it on an oiled cutting board, using a rolling pin for an even 1/4 inch thickness.

Then, I just grab a biscuit cutter, and voila...perfectly round sliders!

Luau Pork

Serves:50 **Prep Time:** 12 Hours Cook **Time:** 12 Hours

Ingredients
- 2 - boneless pork shoulders (6 lbs.)
- 2 C hot water
- 3 Qtrs. gal Hawaiian Mojo
- 2 Tbsp. seasoned salt
- ¼ C Stubbs liquid smoke
- 4 Tbsp. garlic powder
- ½ C Adobo Criollo spices

Directions
1. Marinate pork in Hawaiian Mojo overnight. Remove from marinade, pat dry, and inject each shoulder with 6-8ozs of remaining marinade.

2. Score pork on all sides, rub with salt, then brush with liquid smoke, and sprinkle with garlic. Wrap completely in Ti/Banana leaves, tie with string.

3. Heat one side of your pellet grill to high, covered.

4. Once pre-heated, place the butts on the "cool" side of the grill, roast 3 hours with oak pellets, and then remove banana leaves. Baste with mojo every 45 minutes throughout the rest of the cooking time. The shoulders should not be over any exposed flame.

5. Cover the grill and vent slightly. Slow cook the shoulders for a total of 6 to 8 hours, until the meat is very tender, or you reach 195 F on the meat thermometer.

6. Chop the meat and then mix with a wash of 1/2 cup liquid smoke, 4 cups hot water, 1/4 cup Adobo Criollo spices, and 2 Tbsp. seasoned salt.

7. Let that sit about 15 minutes, drain remaining liquid, and serve with Sweet Hawaiian Pork Sauce .

Carolina Pork Ribs

Serves: 6 **Prep Time:** 12 Hours Cook **Time:** 3 Hours

Ingredients
- 2 racks of pork spareribs
- ½ C of "Burning' Love" Rub
- 1 C Carolina Basting Sauce
- 1 C Carolina BBQ Sauce

Directions
1. Prepare ribs by removing the membrane from the underside. Trim off any loose fat, and season ribs with rub, wrap in plastic wrap and refrigerate overnight.
2. Allow ribs to warm 1 hour. Preheat pellet grill to 280F.
3. Place ribs, bone sides down, on the pellet grill rack over a pan. Cover and grill for 1-1/2 to 1 3/4 hours or until ribs are tender.
4. Remove pan and place ribs directly on pellet grill, turning and brushing with mop sauce every 10 minutes for 30-40 minutes.
5. If you want to sauce the ribs, do so 5 minutes before they're done, turning ever minute, and watch carefully.

Italian Pancetta Sandwiches

Serves: 24 **Prep Time:** 48 Hours Cook **Time:** 8 Hours

Ingredients
- 2 - 8lbs. pork shoulders, butterflied
- 6 Tbsp. fennel Seeds
- 24 cloves garlic, peeled
- Salt & pepper
- 12 Tbsp. fresh rosemary
- 2 C red wine
- 32 oz sliced pancetta
- 24 crusty Italian rolls
- 4 C caramelized onions
- 6 C Italian parsley

Directions
1. Place the fennel, garlic, rosemary, salt, pepper, wine, and pancetta in a food processor and pulse until well mixed.
2. Spread the pancetta mixture evenly over the opened pork butt. Roll the pork up firmly, and tie with kitchen twine in four places to hold the pork together.
3. Wrap in aluminum foil and place in the refrigerator for two days.
4. You want indirect heat for cooking, you can easily do this on a conventional pellet grill.
5. Just keep the meat as far from the heat source as possible, or it will burn during the long cooking time. You want to cook at 250 degrees Fahrenheit; you can go as high as 275, but no higher.
6. Put the shoulder on the "cool side" of the grill and place a disposable pan with a couple of cups of apple juice underneath it.

7. A spray bottle with 50/50 apple juice and cider vinegar is nice for basting, as well.

8. I like to use apple pellets for smoking.

9. After three to four hours, remove the shoulder from your grill, wrap in foil, and roast in a pre-heated oven at 250d for 3-4 hours.

10. The pork is done when it reaches an internal temperature of 195 degrees.

11. If you don't have an instant read thermometer (you should really get one) the meat is done when it pulls apart easily with a fork.

12. Heat the rolls. Place ¼ cup of meat on the warm roll and spoon over a little of the pan juices onto the sandwich.

13. Top meat with caramelized onions, the ¼ cup of fresh chopped parsley.

Bourbon Pork Tenderloin

Serves: 10 **Prep Time:** 24 Hours Cook **Time:** 1 Hour

Ingredients

- 2 C white sugar
- ½ C Jim Beam® Bourbon
- 2 C water
- 2 tsp vanilla extract
- 3 to 4 lbs. pork tenderloin
- 2 tsp black pepper
- 2 tsp garlic powder
- 2 Tbsp. salt

Directions

1. In medium bowl, combine sugar, Jim Beam® Bourbon, water, salt and vanilla. Mix well. Place tenderloin in a large zip bag and pour ½ of marinade over the top. Refrigerate 24 hours. Season tenderloin with garlic and pepper.

2. Heat your pellet grill for two-zone grilling and brush the grill with vegetable oil.

3. Remove the tenderloin from the bag and spoon half of sugar mixture over tenderloins. Place on the "hot" side of the pellet grill and brown to your liking (I like a slight char, about 15 minutes per side.)

4. Move to the "cool" slide of the grate. Cover and cook for 12 to 15 minutes, turning every 1 1/2 to 2 minutes, until the tenderloin reaches an internal temperature of 140 degrees F. Remove the tenderloin from the grill and place on a large piece of heavy-duty aluminum foil folded at the edges to create a basket, and pour on the reserved marinade. Wrap tightly and rest for 10 minutes.

5. Remove to a cutting board and slice against the grain.

Carolina Pulled Pork Sandwiches

Serves: 30 **Prep Time:** 24 Hours Cook **Time:** 12 Hour

Ingredients
- 1 boneless pork butt (5-6 pounds)
- 2 Tbsp. smoked paprika
- 2 Tbsp. hickory salt
- 1 Tbsp. black pepper
- 2 cups cider vinegar
- 1 cup Southern Comfort
- 1 cup water
- 2 Tbsp. molasses
- 2 Tbsp. salt
- ¼ cup hot sauce
- 1 Tbsp. red pepper flakes
- 1 Tbsp. black pepper
- 2 teaspoons ground cayenne

Directions
1. In a bowl, combine paprika, hickory salt, 1 Tbsp. black pepper, and cayenne. Coat pork shoulder with seasonings and cover with plastic wrap. Refrigerate 24 hours.
2. Preheat pellet grill to medium heat. Place pork shoulder on grill and smoke using hickory pellets. Place a grill thermometer on the grate to track temperature. Combine remaining ingredients for baste.
3. Bring pellet grill/smoker to medium temperature (between 225 - 250°F.)
4. Smoke pork shoulder for 6-8 hours.

5. Baste and wrap shoulder in a double layer of foil, place in a pan and return to smoker (or oven) at 225F. Continue cooking to an internal temperature of 185°F.

6. Remove from heat and allow to rest 20 minutes (still in foil) and then unwrap and rest another 10 minutes. Shred pork, tossing with reserved pan juices.

7. Serve on soft white rolls, topped with your favorite coleslaw.

BBQ Sauce Pork Chops

Serves: 6 **Prep Time:** 4 Hours Cook **Time:** 15 Minutes

Ingredients
- 6 boneless pork chops, thick
- 1 Tbsp. salt and sugar
- Pepper to taste
- 1 cup water
- 1 cup sweet barbecue sauce
- 1/4 cup cider vinegar

Directions
1. Place chops in a baggie with 1 cup of water and sugar (boiled and cooled), and brine 4 hours.

2. Preheat your pellet grill for high heat.

3. In a small saucepan, combine barbecue sauce and vinegar. Bring to a simmer and allow to cook 20-30 minutes, uncovered, stirring often.

4. Brush grate lightly with oil before placing pork chops on the grill. Cook over high heat for 10 to 12 minutes, turning once. Brush with sauce just before removing chops from grill.

5. Serve with remaining sauce.

Peach Mojo Pork Shoulder

Serves: 12 **Prep Time:** 1 Hours Cook **Time:** 6 hours

Ingredients
- 1 - 6lbs. pork shoulder
- 1 qt Hawaiian Mojo (see recipe)
- ½ cup sea-salt
- 1 can peach slices, in syrup
- 2 Tbsp. garlic powder
- 2 Tbsp. red pepper flakes
- 15 oz sliced peaches in syrup
- 16 oz peach preserves
- 12oz apricot & pineapple preserves
- ½ cup Stubbs Mesquite Liquid Smoke

Directions
1. Inject the pork with mojo and marinate overnight. Then, allow pork to come to room temp just before roasting.
2. Brush pork liberally with liquid smoke, then rub all over with sea-salt, garlic, and 1 Tbsp. of red pepper flakes. Let rest 1 hour.
3. Glaze: Combine liquid smoke, canned peaches (with syrup), apricot/pineapple preserves, peach preserves, and remaining red pepper flakes. Simmer one hour over medium-low heat.
4. Cool to room temp.
5. Preheat pellet grill for medium heat (225-250F). Place pork shoulder on grill and smoke using hickory pellets.
6. Smoke pork shoulder for 5-6 hours or until internal temperatures reach 185°F.
7. Use baste every 20 minutes during the last three hours of cooking.

8. Remember to boil any remaining basting sauce before using it on the pork.

9. Slice the pork and pile in a pan, slather the top with a generous layer of peach-pineapple glaze and then place pans under a hot broiler for another 5-10 minutes to brown the glaze.

10. Serve with sweet Hawaiian rolls and white rice.

Sweet & Savory Bacon Wrapped Dates

Serves: 16 **Prep Time:** 30 Minutes Cook **Time:** 30 Minutes

Ingredients
- 1 lb. thick-sliced bacon, cut in half
- 1 lb. pitted dates
- 4 ounces gorgonzola cheese
- 32 toothpicks

Directions
1. Slice dates up one side and open them up. Pinch off a piece of cheese and place it into the center of the date.
2. Close the halves of the dates and wrap a half-slice of bacon around the outside, secure with a toothpick.
3. Lay a single sheet of foil over pellet grill grates and add the wraps in a single layer.
4. Grill until bacon starts to crisp, then flip each wrap over.
5. When the second side is crisped, remove to a platter lined with paper towels, allow to cool slightly before serving.

Jalapeño Pepper Bombs

Serves: 10 **Prep Time:** 10 Minutes Cook **Time:** 15 Minutes

Ingredients
- 10 fresh jalapenos
- 20 Cheddar Little Smokies
- 8oz. Cream Cheese
- 2 lbs. Bacon (½ strip each)
- 1/8 Sweet Onion (diced)

- 1 Tbsp. Sugar

Directions

1. Soften cream cheese and blend in sugar and onions.

2. Slice Jalapenos in half, lengthwise, and trim away all seeds and membranes, rinse.

3. Spoon 1 teaspoon of cream cheese mixture into each side. Place 1 smokie on each half and press it into the cream cheese.

4. Wrap each pepper half in bacon, securing each with a toothpick, oil and heat one side of your pellet grill to medium heat.

5. Add the bombs in a single layer. Grill until bacon starts to crisp, moving to coll side of the grill starts flaring up, and then remove to a platter lined with paper towels.

6. Allow to cool slightly and serve.

If these "bombs" have too little kick heat for you, use a whole pepper for each. Clamshell the cream cheese and smokie in the pepper and wrap the whole wonderful thing in bacon.

Fish & Seafood

Simple Grilled Oysters

Serves: 8 **Prep Time:** 10 Minutes Cook **Time:** 5 Minutes

Ingredients
- 4 dozen oysters, scrubbed
- Lemon wedges
- 1 C butter
- 1 Tsp seasoned salt
- 1 tsp lemon pepper

Directions
1. Preheat pellet grill to 350F.
2. Melt butter with seasoned salt and lemon pepper, mixing well. Simmer 10 minutes.
3. Place oysters, unshelled, on pellet grill.
4. Oysters have a "cup" side (like a bowl) and a "lid" side (flat), the cup side should be down so as not to lose all the yummy juices.
5. When shells pop open (3-5 minutes), use an oyster knife to detach oyster from top shell, and plop it back into the cup with the hot oyster liquor. Discard the lid.
6. Add a teaspoon of seasoned butter and serve.
7. Oysters that don't open should be discarded.

Garlic Asiago Oysters

Serves: 12 **Prep Time:** 10 Minutes Cook **Time:** 5 Minutes

Ingredients
- 1 lb. sweet cream butter
- 1 Tbsp. minced garlic
- 2 dozen fresh oysters
- ½ C. grated Asiago cheese
- French bread, warmed
- ¼ cup chives, diced

Directions
1. Start pellet grill and heat to medium high.

2. Melt butter over medium-high heat. Reduce heat to low and stir in garlic.

3. Cook 1 minute and remove from heat.

4. Place oysters, cup down, on pellet grill. As soon as shells pop open, remove from grill.

5. Shuck oysters, keeping as much of the oyster liquor in place as possible.

6. Cut connective muscle and return each oyster to its shell.

7. Drizzle each oyster with 2 teaspoons butter mixture and sprinkle with 1 teaspoon cheese. Grill over high heat 3 minutes or until cheese browns. Sprinkle with chives.

8. Remove from pellet grill and serve immediately with bread and remaining butter on the side.

Wasabi Oysters

Serves: 6 **Prep Time:** 20 Minutes Cook **Time:** 5 Minutes

Ingredients
- 12 small Pacific oysters, raw in shell 2 Tbsp. white wine vinegar
- 8 oz white wine 1/4 C shallots, minced
- 2 Tbsp. wasabi mustard 1 Tbsp. soy sauce
- 1 C unsalted butter, cubed 1 C chopped cilantro leaves
- salt and black pepper to taste

Directions
1. In a saucepan, over medium heat, combine the white wine vinegar, wine and shallots. Simmer until the liquid is slightly reduced. Strain out shallots and discard, return liquid to the pan. Reduce heat to low. Add wasabi mustard and soy sauce, stirring.

2. Over low heat, gradually whisk in butter. Do not let the mixture boil. When all of the butter has been incorporated, stir in cilantro, and remove from heat. Pour into a small bowl and set aside.

3. Prepare a dish of coarse salt to hold the oyster shells in place.

4. Clean oysters thoroughly. Place oysters, flat side up, on the pellet grill preheated to medium, and close the lid. Cook oysters until shells just open (5-6 minutes). Remove oysters from the pellet grill and cut the connective muscle from the top shell, (careful – don't spill the liquor.) Turn the oyster over and return it to the cup half of shell. Discard the lid.

5. Press each oyster (in shell) into the coarse salt to keep it upright, then spoon 1-2 teaspoons of wasabi-butter sauce over each and serve immediately.

6. Be prepared to cook a lot of oysters!

Fish Camp Trout

Serves: 2 **Prep Time:** 5 Minutes Cook **Time:** 15 Minutes

Ingredients
- 4 small whole trout, cleaned
- 4 strips of bacon
- 4 sprigs of fresh thyme
- 1 lemon
- salt and pepper to taste

Directions
1. Oil grates and preheat pellet grill. Fry bacon, so that it's started to cook, but is still soft. Rinse out the trout and pat dry with a paper towel.

2. Place a sprig of thyme inside each fish. Wrap each trout with a strip of bacon and secure with a toothpick.

3. Place trout on pellet grill or in an oiled grill basket, and grill 5-7 minutes per side depending on the size of the trout. The trout is done when the meat turns opaque in the center and easily flakes.

4. Squeeze a little fresh lemon juice over each fish and serve.

Southern-Grilled Bass

Serves: 4 **Prep Time:** 5 Minutes Cook **Time:** 15 Minutes

Ingredients
- 2 lbs. bass fillets or steaks
- 1 C. mayonnaise
- 4 oz. soy sauce

Directions
1. Mix mayonnaise and soy sauce.

2. Cover entire surface (meat side) of each bass fillet with mixture.

3. Place on pellet grill, skin-side down. Do not turn.

4. When edges turn up and scales flake, remove and serve.

Pacific Northwest Salmon

with Lemon Dill Sauce

Serves: 8 **Prep Time:** 5 Minutes Cook **Time:** 15 Minutes

Ingredients
- 6lb Chinook salmon fillets
- Salt to taste
- 1 C butter, melted
- 1 C lemon juice
- 4 Tbsp. dried dill weed
- 1 Tbsp. garlic salt
- Black pepper to taste
- 4 C plain yogurt

Directions
1. Place salmon fillets in a baking dish.
2. Mix the butter and 1/2 lemon juice in a small bowl, and drizzle over the salmon. Season with salt & pepper.
3. Combine yogurt, dill, garlic powder, sea salt, and pepper. Spread sauce evenly over salmon.
4. Quickly wipe hot pellet grill grate with a towel dipped in a little canola oil, place fillets on grill, tent with foil, and close lid.
5. Grill fish, skin down, to medium rare, about 6 minutes. (Fish should be well colored on the outside and barely translucent at the center.) or until salmon is easily flaked with a fork.
6. Plate and spoon extra sauce over the top.
7. Serve with wild rice.

Seared Wasabi Tuna

Serves: 8 **Prep Time:** 5 Minutes Cook **Time:** 3 Minutes

Ingredients
- 6-ounce tuna steaks
- 1 1/4 cup white wine
- 1 cup cilantro leaves
- 1 cup unsalted butter
- 1/4 cup shallots, minced
- 2 Tbsp. white wine vinegar
- 1 tablespoon wasabi paste
- 1 tablespoon soy sauce
- 1 tablespoon olive oil
- salt and pepper to taste

Directions
1. Combine wine, wine vinegar and shallots in a saucepan over medium heat. Simmer to reduce to about 2 tablespoons. Strain out the shallots and discard.
2. Add wasabi and soy sauce to mixture and reduce the heat. Slowly add butter while stirring until completely mixed. Stir in cilantro and remove from heat. Set aside.
3. Preheat pellet grill as hot as you can get it. You really need a lot of heat for this one.
4. Brush tuna steaks with olive oil. Season with salt and pepper and place on grill.
5. Grill for 90 seconds then turn and continue grilling for 90 seconds more. If you just want the tuna seared remove from grill now. Otherwise continue grilling for 1 minute on each side again.
6. Serve with sauce.

Bacon Grilled Crappie

Serves: 5 **Prep Time:** 10 Minutes Cook **Time:** 3 Minutes

Ingredients
- 20 Crappie Fillets
- 20 Bacon Slices
- ¼ teaspoon garlic powder
- ¼ teaspoon onion powder
- ¼ teaspoon pepper

Directions
1. Sprinkle spices on fillets. Roll up fillets, wrap with bacon and peg with a toothpick.

2. Grill over very low heat, with apple wood pellets, turning fillets several times.

3. Be sure to put out all flames caused by bacon grease with a water spray bottle.

4. Cook until bacon is brown and inside of fillet flakes.

Mojo Shrimp Skewer Appetizers

Serves: 32 **Prep Time:** 10 Minutes Cook **Time:** 6 Minute

Ingredients
- 2 lbs. sliced bacon
- 64 raw prawns, tail off
- 2 C Traditional Cuban Mojo
- ¼ C Adobo Criollo
- 32 wood skewers, soaked

Directions
1. Rinse raw prawns and drain. In a large bowl, toss prawns and Adobo Criollo spices.

2. Wrap each prawn in ½ slice of bacon, and thread two wraps onto each skewer, touching, and with skewer through both the bacon and the shrimp.

3. Bring pellet grill to medium heat, oil, and lay skewers in grill.

4. Grill 3-5 minutes, until bacon is cooked, flip, and cook 2-3 more minutes.

Remove from grill and let rest on a paper-towel covered platters 2-3 minutes before serving. for this type of grilling.

Sweet Grilled Lobster Tails

Serves: 12 **Prep Time:** 10 Minutes Cook **Time:** 7 Minutes

Ingredients
- 12 lobster tails
- ½ C olive oil
- ¼ C fresh lemon juice
- ½ C butter
- 1 Tbsp. crushed garlic
- 1 tsp sugar
- 1/2 tsp salt
- ½ tsp black pepper

Directions
1. Combine lemon juice, butter, garlic, salt, and pepper over med-low heat and mix until well blended, keep warm.
2. Create a "cool zone" at one end of the pellet grill. Brush the meat side of tails with olive oil, place onto grill and cook for 5-7 minutes, depending on the size of the lobster tail.
3. Make sure to turn once during cooking process.
4. After turning, baste meat with garlic butter 2-3 times.
5. The shell should be bright red when they are finished. Remove the tails from the grill, and using large kitchen shears, cut the top part of the shell open.
6. Serve with warm garlic butter for dipping.

Sturgeon Kabobs

Serves: 32 **Prep Time:** 80 Minutes Cook **Time:** 10 Minutes

Ingredients
- 4 lbs. raw sturgeon
- 4 lbs. sliced bacon
- 12 metal double-skewers
- 2 bottles of Teriyaki sauce
- 4 cans pineapple chunks (optional)

Directions
1. Cut sturgeon into 1-inch cubes. Wrap a half slice of bacon around it, and skewer, making sure to pin the bacon, as well as the meat, (so the bacon won't fall off.)

2. Alternate pineapple and bacon wrapped sturgeon, until skewers are full.

3. Place filled skewers in a baking dish and pour the teriyaki sauce over them, turning to coat well, and let sit for 1 hour.

4. Place skewers on your pellet grill, over high heat, and baste with sauce while cooking.

5. Cook 8-10 minutes, turning and re-basting once. Do not allow the bacon to burn.

If you're using wooden skewers, make sure you soak them for about 20 minutes before grilling.

Grilled Clams

Serves: 4 **Prep Time:** 10 Minutes Cook **Time:** 10 Minutes

Ingredients
- 2 dozen sm. Cockle, littleneck
- 1 cup olive oil
- 1 pound sweet butter, melted
- 1 lemon, juiced
- 2 tsp fresh minced garlic
- 2 tsp minced Italian parsley

Directions
1. Inspect the cockles to ensure the shells are closed. Since clams live in sand, they need to be thoroughly rinsed under cold water several times to rid the shell of debris.
2. Combine butter, lemon juice, garlic and parsley in food processor, keep warm beside your pellet grill.
3. Grill clams over medium heat. Cover with foil or close the grill lid and steam the clams 2-3 minutes, checking often, until the shells have just popped open.
4. Dredge each open clam in the butter mixture and set back on the grill.
5. Cook 1-2 minutes longer.
6. Plate cockles and add salt.

Poultry

Spatchcocked Garlic Chicken

Serves: 4 **Prep Time:** 12 Hours Cook **Time:** 40 Minutes

Ingredients
- 1 - 4 pound young chicken 1 Tbsp. sea salt
- 2 Tsp ground pepper 4 Tbsp. olive oil
- 4 cloves minced garlic

Directions
1. Place chicken breast side down and using poultry shears cut out the backbone. Spread the two sides apart and press down on the breast so that the chicken lies flat.

2. Combine olive oil, garlic, and pepper.

3. Wash the chicken in cold water, and pat dry. Rub chicken with oil/spice blend and drop into a gallon-size plastic bag. Refrigerate overnight.

4. Heat one side of pellet grill to high, cover and preheat for 20 minutes.

5. Place chicken skin side down on the "cool" side, with legs closest to the heat. Watch carefully and turn over when skin starts to brown. Cover with a large disposable aluminum pan (a favorite restaurant trick.)

6. Cooking time will vary, depending on the heat and the size of the chicken. Check the temperature at 20 minutes after turning.

7. When the temperature in the thigh reaches 175, remove from the heat and let sit, covered, for 15 minutes before carving.

Beer Can Chicken

Serves: 4 **Prep Time:** 12 Hours Cook **Time:** 60 Minutes

Ingredients
- 1 large whole chicken (4 to 5 pounds)
- 3 tablespoons rub (recipe below)
- 1 12-ounce can of beer

Directions
1. Rinse the chicken, inside and out, under cold running water; then drain and pat dry. Rub 1 tablespoon of the rub inside the body cavity; then another tablespoon all over the skin. Rub another half-tablespoon between the flesh and the skin.

2. Cover and refrigerate the chicken overnight.

3. Open a can of beer. Pour out a couple of inches of beer; then, using a screw driver, carefully poke several holes around the top of the can.

4. Pour remaining dry rub into the can.

5. Holding the chicken upright (legs pointed down), insert the beer can up into the chicken. Insert junior-high boy's locker-room humor here.

6. Oil the pellet grill grate. Stand the chicken up in the center of the hot grate, over the drip pan. Spread out the legs to form a tripod, to support the bird.

7. Cover the pellet grill and cook the chicken about an hour. Use a thermometer to check for doneness. The internal temperature should be a minimum 170 degrees.

8. Using tongs, lift the bird to a cutting board or platter, allowing the beer can to slip out onto the grill. Be careful, the contents of the can are VERY hot. An assistant with a second set of tongs is helpful here.

9. Let stand for 5 minutes before carving.

Beer-Can Chicken Rub

This is a simple, easy to make rub that is pretty darn good with just about anything. You rub enough of this on an old boot, and it wouldn't be half bad.

Ingredients
- 1/4 cup coarse sea salt
- 1/2 cup light brown sugar
- 1/4 cup smoked paprika
- 2 tablespoons freshly ground black pepper

Directions
1. Combine all ingredients and mix with your fingers. Store the rub in an airtight jar away from heat and light. Good for at least 6 months.
2. Makes about 1 cup

Flattened Mojo Chicken

Serves: 12 **Prep Time:** 24 Hours Cook **Time:** 60 Minutes

Ingredients
- 3 - 4lb whole chickens 3 Tbsp. olive oil
- 6 C Traditional Cuban Mojo 3 tsp. sea salt
- 3 Tbsp. Adobo Criollo spices

Directions
1. Rinse chicken with cold water and pat dry. Cut out backbone with kitchen shears.

2. Turn chicken breast side up and open like a book. Press down firmly on breast to flatten and break rib bones. Loosen skin from body under breast and thighs.

3. Place each chicken in a gallon-size resealable bag with 2 cups Mojo. Marinate (flat) in refrigerator 24 hours. Remove chickens from bags and discard mojo. Blot each bird dry, and rub each with 1 Tbsp. olive oil, and then 1 Tbsp. Adobo Criollo spice blend.

4. Pre-heat one side of your pellet grill; and leave one side unlighted, cover and preheat for 20 minutes. Place chicken skin side down in the middle of the grill with legs closest to the heat.

5. Watch carefully and turn over when skin starts to brown. Turn and move chicken to the "cool" side and cover with a large disposable aluminum pan (a favorite restaurant trick.)

6. Cooking time will vary, depending on the fire and the size of the chicken. Check the temperature at 20 minutes after turning. When the temperature in the thigh reaches 175 degrees, remove from the heat and let sit, loosely covered for 15 minutes.

7. Halve, quarter, or carve the chicken and serve with Saffron Basmati Rice

Lazy Chicken Legs

Serves: 8 **Prep Time:** 12 Hours Cook **Time:** 20 Minutes

Ingredients
- 1 "Family Pack" Chicken legs or thighs
- 1 bottle Yoshida's Original (or your favorite Oriental grilling sauce.)

Directions
1. Combine chicken and sauce in a gallon-size resealable bag and allow to marinate 8-12 hours, turning several times.

2. Start a two-zone cooking surface on your pellet grill, with a cool area in the middle.

3. Grill chicken over hot-zones until browned on both sides, then move to cool area, and cover with foil pan.

4. Cook, turning once until done, 10-15 minutes.

5. Serve with sticky rice and stir-fly veggies.

This recipe is awesome with boneless chicken thighs, too. When cooked, just slice and serve as a rice bowl. Boil the marinade 10-15 minutes, stirring, and top!

Competition BBQ Chicken

Serves: 8 **Prep Time:**10 Minutes Cook **Time:** 40 Minutes

Ingredients
- 2 whole chickens, cut up
- ¼ cup olive oil
- 2 tsp salt
- 1 cup bottled BBQ sauce
- ¼ cup cider vinegar
- ¼ cup brown sugar, packed
- 2 Tbsp. hot sauce

Directions
1. Clean the chicken and prepare the grill. Brush chicken pieces with olive oil and season with salt.

2. Heat one side of your pellet grill to medium high heat, and place chicken skin side down directly over heat. Grill until the skin is seared; turn and sear the other side. Keep the pellet grill covered while cooking but watch for flare-ups. Keep a spray bottle handy.

3. When both sides are seared, remove chicken to the "cool" side of the pellet grill to finish cooking over indirect heat.

4. Brush the chicken with sauce.

5. Turn every 10 minutes or so and brush with sauce again until the chicken is done with an internal temperature of about 160° F.

6. Boneless breasts will cook thoroughly in only 15-20 minutes. Meaty, bone-in pieces will require 35-45 minutes of cooking over medium-low heat.

7. When the chicken is done, place over direct heat for a few minutes to caramelize the sauce and add deeper color if desired.

Sizzling' Buffalo Wings

Serves: 8 **Prep Time:**10 Minutes Cook **Time:** 40 Minutes

Ingredients
- 36 chicken wings, separated
- 1 Tbsp. vegetable oil
- 1 tsp salt
- 1 C all-purpose flour
- 1 ½ Tbsp. white vinegar
- ¼ tsp cayenne pepper
- ¼ tsp garlic powder
- 1 tsp Tabasco sauce
- ¼ tsp Worcestershire sauce
- ¼ tsp seasoned salt
- 6 Tbsp. Frank's Red Hot Sauce
- 6 Tbsp. unsalted butter
- celery sticks blue cheese dressing

Directions
1. Mix all except chicken, salt, oil and flour in a pan, bring to a simmer, stirring, and then cool.
2. Toss the wings with the oil, and salt. Place into a large plastic bag, add the flour, and shake to coat evenly. Remove from the bag, shaking off excess flour.
3. Place wings on hot pellet grill, turning several times until golden brown.
4. Remove wings from grill and place them in a sealed bowl with the sauce and shake well.
5. Serve immediately with blue cheese and chilled celery sticks.

Peanut Chicken Satays

Serves: 8 **Prep Time:**12 Hours Cook **Time:** 40 Minutes

Ingredients
- 4 Tbsp. olive oil
- 4 Tbsp. sesame oil
- 2 tsp ginger powder
- 2 tsp powdered garlic
- 2 Tbsp. curry powder Butter lettuce leaves
- 20 wooden skewers, soaked Fresh cilantro leaves
- 2 lbs. chicken thighs, cut into strips

Peanut sauce:
- 2 C chunky peanut butter
- ½ C soy sauce
- 1/4 C brown sugar
- ¼ C sweet chili paste
- 1/3 C limes juice
- 2/3 C hot water

Directions
1. Combine oils, ginger, garlic, and curry powder in a shallow mixing bowl. Place the chicken strips in the marinade and gently toss until well coated. Cover and let the chicken marinate in the refrigerator overnight.

2. Thread the chicken pieces onto the soaked skewers working the skewer in and out of the meat, down the middle of the piece, so that it stays in place during grilling.

3. Brush pellet grill with oil to prevent the meat from sticking. Grill the satays for 3 to 5 minutes on each side, until nicely seared and cooked through.

4. Serve on a platter lined with lettuce leaves and cilantro; accompanied by a small bowl of peanut sauce on the side.

For the sauce:
5. Combine the peanut butter, soy sauce, chili paste, brown sugar, and lime juice in a food processor or blender. Puree to combine, and drizzle in the hot water to thin out the sauce. Pour the sauce into individual serving bowls.

If you're serving this as a main dish, add a side of steamed jasmine rice, and fresh veggies.

Sauces, Rubs, & Mops

North Carolina Barbecue Sauce

In the Carolinas, the barbeque meat is pork, and the barbeque sauces are matters of hot debate even from one town to the next. Some sauces are thin and vinegary, while some regions add ketchup, or even mustard. This is the recipe I grew up with.

Ingredients
- 1 qt cider vinegar
- 12 oz ketchup
- 2/3 C packed brown sugar
- 2 Tbsp. salt
- ¼ C lemon juice
- 1 Tbsp. red pepper flakes
- 1 Tbsp. smoked paprika
- 1 Tbsp. onion powder
- 1 tsp each: black pepper, dry mustard

Directions
1. Bring all ingredients to the boil, and then simmer for 30-45 minutes, stirring frequently.
2. Allow to cool and serve or bottle.

Memphis-Style Barbecue Sauce

Memphis barbecue sauce has its own distinctive flavor, as well. Though the specific ingredients will vary from cook to cook, Memphis sauce is usually made with tomatoes, vinegar, and any countless combination of spices.

Ingredients
- 1 Tbsp. butter
- ¼ C finely chopped onion
- 1 ½ C ketchup
- ¼ C chili sauce
- 4 Tbsp. brown sugar
- 4 Tbsp. molasses
- 2 Tbsp. yellow mustard
- 1 Tbsp. fresh lemon juice
- 1 Tbsp. Worcestershire sauce
- 1 Tbsp. liquid hickory smoke
- ½ tsp garlic powder
- ½ tsp salt
- ½ tsp ground black pepper
- 1 tsp chili powder
- dash cayenne pepper

Directions
1. Bring all ingredients to the boil, and then simmer for 30-45 minutes, stirring frequently.
2. Allow to cool and serve or bottle.

Texas Brisket Sauce

Texas is famous for tender slow-smoked brisket. Sauces are usually thin, spicy, and mixed with intensely flavorful pan drippings.

Ingredients
- ½ C brisket drippings (defatted)
- ½ C vinegar
- 1 Tbsp. Worcestershire sauce
- ½ C ketchup
- ½ tsp hot pepper sauce (Franks)
- 1 lg onion, diced
- 2 cloves of garlic, pressed
- 1 Tbsp. salt
- ½ tsp chili powder
- Juice of one lemon

Directions
1. Combine all ingredients.
2. Simmer, stirring occasionally, for 15 minutes.
3. Allow to cool and refrigerate 24-48 hours before using.

Sweet Hawaiian Pork Sauce

Kalua Pork (or pig) is one of my favorite Hawaiian dishes. It's a smoky, salty pulled pork dish served over white rice, with a variety of optional sauces - from a simple liquid smoke and water wash, to elaborate sauces that highlight the tropical fruits and sugar cane of the islands.

Ingredients
- 15oz peaches & juice
- 15oz pineapple & juice
- 16oz peach preserves
- 1 cup brown sugar
- 2 Tbsp. liquid smoke
- 2 Tbsp. minced garlic
- 1 Tbsp. red pepper flakes

Directions
1. Combine all and bring to boil.

2. Lower heat and simmer on low until sauce has begun to thicken.

3. Keep warm until serving. Drizzle over pulled pork.

For a very classy presentation, shred the pork, top with whole pineapple rings, baste well with sauce, sprinkle generously with crushed macadamia nuts, and return to you pellet grill 5-10 minutes to brown the top.

Spicy Thai Peanut Sauce

Ingredients
- 3 C creamy peanut butter
- 3/4 C coconut milk
- 1/3 C fresh lime juice
- 1/3 C soy sauce
- 1 Tbsp. fish sauce
- 1 Tbsp. hot sauce
- 1 Tbsp. minced fresh ginger root
- 5 cloves garlic. minced

Directions
1. In a bowl, mix the peanut butter, coconut milk, lime juice, soy sauce, fish sauce, hot sauce, ginger, and garlic.
2. Simmer 10 minutes, cool and serve.

Garlic Mojo

Ingredients
- 8 garlic cloves
- 1 tsp salt
- 1/4 C sweet orange juice
- 1/8 C of fresh lime or lemon juice.
- 1 Habanero pepper, diced (optional)

Directions
1. Chop garlic fine with salt, or crush using a mortar and pestle or food processor with salt to form a thick paste.

2. Wearing gloves, carefully core Habanero pepper and wash out all seeds and membranes. Dice pepper, set aside. Wash prep area, dispose of gloves and wash your hands with dish soap.

3. In a mixing bowl, combine the garlic paste, pepper, and juice, and let the mixture sit at room temperature for 30 minutes or longer.

Gorgonzola Dipping Sauce

Ingredients
- 1 C crumbled blue cheese
- 2/3 C sour cream
- ½ C mayonnaise
- 1 clove garlic, minced
- 1 oz white wine
- 2 tsp Worcestershire sauce
- 1 tsp salt
- 1 tsp fresh ground black pepper

Directions
1. In a glass or plastic bowl, combine all ingredients, using the salt and pepper to finalize the taste and the white wine to set the consistency.

What is a Rub?

In the food of the Southern United States, dry rub is often used on grilled or barbequed meats.

Dry rubbed ribs are a popular dish, but steaks, burgers or pork chops are also given flavor through a spice rub.

Most typical Southern style spice rubs include chili and cayenne pepper, garlic and onion powder, salt and black pepper, paprika and dry mustard.

Although the quantities of hot ingredients can be adjusted, rubs are often an extremely spicy mix that add a powerful kick to meat.

"Burning' Love" Rub

This is my secret pork shoulder rub. Apply it generously to the inside of a butterflied shoulder, roll it, tie it, and apply more rub to the outside. You MUST allow the rubbed shoulder to rest in the fridge at least overnight so that the rub will help form that wonderful "bark" while roasting.

Finally, after it's done cooking and you've pulled, chopped, or shredded the meat, give it one last sprinkle for an intense, spicy flavor.

Ingredients
- ¼ C coarse sea salt
- ¼ C light brown sugar
- 2 Tbsp. garlic powder
- 2 Tbsp. onion powder
- 2 Tbsp. Italian seasonings
- 4 Tbsp. smoked paprika
- 2 Tbsp. course black pepper
- 1 Tbsp. hickory salt
- 1 tsp cayenne powder

Directions
1. Combine and mix well.
2. Good for 6-8lbs. of pork.

Brisket Rub

Ingredients
- (For 4 full briskets 7-8lbs. each)
- 1 C fine sea salt
- 1 C coarse pepper
- 1 C granulated garlic
- 1/4 C smoked paprika

Directions
1. Rub briskets and refrigerate 12-24 hours.

2. Allow briskets to come to room temp before smoking.

3. Smoke brisket(s) with a combination of oak and pecan wood pellets, at a temp between 225-250.

The difference between good brisket and amazing brisket is patience.

Double wrap the finishing brisket in foil, wrap that in a towel, and let the whole thing rest in a closed cooler for 1-2 hours.

Then, once you've unwrapped it, allow it to sit and cool slightly for 15-20 minutes for slicing or pulling.

Smokey Beef Rib Rub

Ingredients

- 2 Tbsp. brown sugar
- 2 Tbsp. black pepper
- 2 Tbsp. smoked paprika
- 2 Tbsp. chili powder
- 2 tsp onion salt
- 2 tsp garlic powder
- 2 tsp celery salt
- 2 tsp seasoning salt

Instructions

1. Mix well and rub both sides of ribs, wrap tightly in plastic wrap, and refrigerate overnight.

2. Bring ribs to room temperature before cooking.

Hellfire Cajun Rub

Ingredients
- 8 Tbsp. smoked paprika
- 4 Tbsp. cayenne powder
- 4 Tbsp. dried parsley
- 4 Tbsp. black pepper
- 2 Tbsp. garlic powder
- 6 Tbsp. fine sea salt
- 2 Tbsp. ground cumin
- 4 Tbsp. dried oregano
- 1 tsp ghost chili powder (to taste)

Directions
1. Combine all the ingredients, mix well and store 24-48 hours, in an airtight container, before using.

Note: Wear gloves, and use extreme caution, when handling ghost chili powder, even breathing the tiniest amount will be painful.

This chili has been measured at over 1 million Scoville units (by comparison, Jalapeno peppers are about 4500 Scoville units.)

This is the hottest Chili Powder available anywhere.

Start with just a teaspoon...trust me. ;)

A Word About Mops

Barbecue "Mops" or basting sauces, are vinegar (or other) acid-based liquids that are applied to meats during the slow cooking process of traditional barbecue, to keep the meat moist. Help in muscle breakdown and add to flavor.

Legend has it that President Johnson liked his barbecue, and often called upon is favorite Pitmaster to cook for hundreds of guests.

The meal would be cooked on a forty square-foot open air fire pit. The cook would cover every inch of this in ribs, briskets, halved pigs, and just about any other meat he could think of.

To keep all that meat moist, he mopped it with a thinned sauce...using a real mop. Hence the barbecue term, "mop."

Today you can buy a miniature tool that looks like a kitchen mop to mop your meat. the cotton fibers hold the thin mop sauce and make it easy to dash large amounts on at once.

If you ask the barbecue experts, they'll tell you that rubs and mop sauces are key to every Championship BBQ team.

Carolina Basting Mop

Mopping (basting) the meat while cooking helps keep it moist and adds additional flavors. Never use a basting brush on any meat that has a dry rub applied, as it will brush off seasonings.

Mop the meat every 30 minutes for the first half of the cooking time.

Ingredients
- 2 qtrs. Water
- 2 qtrs. Apple Cider Vinegar
- 2 qtrs. vegetable oil
- 1 C liquid smoke
- ½ C salt
- ¼ C cayenne pepper
- ¼ C black pepper
- 1 sweet onion, diced fine

Directions
1. Combine all ingredients and bring to a simmer.

2. Allow to cool overnight, and warm before using.

3. Use as a rib/chicken baste, or sprinkle on pulled or chopped pork before serving.

Basic Vinegar Mop

Ingredients
- 2 C cider vinegar
- ½ C vegetable oil
- 5 tsp salt
- 4 tsp red pepper flakes or powder

Directions
1. Combine all ingredients and bring to a simmer, allow to cool overnight to help the flavors marry.
2. Keep warm and apply to meat before you close your pellet grill/smoker, when you flip the meat, and again when the meat is done cooking.
3. Allow the meat to rest at least 30 minutes to soak up the mop.

Perry's Pig Picking' Mop

This recipe is for the whole hog, but in reality, it can be used for all types of pork. If you're preparing smaller cuts of pork, simply scale back the quantities. Use as a marinade, and injection, a mop, and finally, as a wash on the finished meat, just before serving.

Ingredients
- 1 qt. apple juice
- 1 qt. apple cider vinegar
- ¼ C fine sea salt
- ¼ C garlic powder
- ¼ C smoked paprika
- 1 C light oil
- 1 tsp black pepper
- 1 tsp cayenne pepper

Directions
1. Simmer for 15-20 minutes.

2. Keep warm and apply to pig before you close your pellet smoker, when you flip the pig, and again when the pig is done cooking.

For a more traditional "Eastern" North Carolina mop, use only the apple juice, vinegar, salt, and cayenne. For South Carolina, add 1 cup prepared mustard to that.

Beef Rib Mop

Ingredients

- 3/4 C brown sugar
- 1/2 C bottled barbecue sauce
- 1/2 C ketchup
- 1/2 C cider vinegar
- 1/2 C Worcestershire sauce
- 1 C water
- 1 Tbsp. salt
- 1 Tbsp. chili powder
- 1 Tbsp. paprika

Directions

1. Combine all ingredients in a quart jar. Shake to blend thoroughly.

2. Best if made ahead of time; will keep indefinitely in the refrigerator.

3. This mop is great for brisket, as well. Keep warm and apply to ribs before you close your pellet smoker, when you flip the ribs, and again when the ribs are done cooking.

Traditional Cuban Mojo

This classic Cuban seasoning sauce makes a flavorful marinade for meats and poultry. Traditionally this is made with sour oranges, cumin, lots of garlic. With larger cuts (pork shoulder, or whole pig & lamb) it can be injected into the meat 12-24 hours before cooking.

Ingredients
- 1 C sour orange juice
- 1 Tbsp. oregano
- 1 Tbsp. bay leaves
- 1 garlic bulb
- 1 tsp cumin
- 3 tsp salt
- 4 oz of water

Directions
1. Peel and mash the garlic cloves. Mix all the ingredients and let it sit for a minimum of one hour.

2. For marinade, add the above recipe to 1 ½ gallons of water, and 13 oz. of table salt.

3. Blend all ingredients and let it sit for a minimum of one hour, strain and inject, or place meat in a cooler and pour marinade to cover overnight.

You can replace the sour orange juice with the following mix: 6 oz. orange juice, 2 oz. lemon juice.

Hawaiian Mojo

I love the sweet, Polynesian overtones that this marinade/mop adds to pork.

Ingredients
- 1 C orange juice
- 1 C pineapple juice
- ½ C mesquite liquid smoke
- 1 Tbsp. oregano
- 1 Tbsp. minced garlic
- 1 tsp cumin
- 3 tsp salt
- 4 oz. of water

Directions
1. Mix all the ingredients and let it sit for a minimum of one hour.
2. For marinade/injection, add the above recipe to 1 ½ gallons of water, and 13 oz. of table salt.
3. Blend all ingredients and let it sit for a minimum of one hour, strain and inject, or place meat in a cooler and pour marinade to cover.
4. Allow to marinate overnight.
5. After injecting/soaking the pig or shoulder, pat dry with paper towels and apply a salt rub all over the meat, use Kosher salt or coarse sea salt.

Resources

Approximate Servings Per Pound

(Raw weight)

- Pork, Shoulder Bone-in 3
- Pork, Back Ribs 1.5
- Pork, Country Style Ribs 2
- Pork, Spareribs 1.5
- Pork, Whole 1.5
- Beef, Standing Rib 2.5
- Beef, Ribs 2.5
- Beef, Tri-Tip 4
- Chicken, Whole 3
- Lamb, Leg (bone in) 1

Turkey, Whole ¾

When planning a meal, it is always better to purchase too much meat than not enough.

Always be prepared for people with larger appetites.

One trick I use is to add a "mystery" guest for every 4 confirmed. In other words, I plan 5 portions for 4 people, 10 portions for 8, 15 for 12, etc.

If there are leftovers, the cooked meat will keep in the refrigerator for several days or the unused portions may be frozen for long term storage.

Wood Smoking Chart

Wood type	Characteristics	Use with
Alder	Very delicate with a hint of sweetness.	Good with fish, pork, poultry, and light-meat game birds. Traditionally used in the Northwest to smoke Salmon
Apple	Slightly sweet but denser, fruity smoke flavor.	Beef, poultry, game birds, pork (particularly ham).
Cherry	Slightly sweet, fruity smoke flavor.	Good with all meats.
Hickory	Pungent, smoky, bacon-like flavor.	Good for all smoking, especially pork and ribs.
Maple	Mildly smoky, somewhat sweet flavor.	Good with pork, poultry, and small game birds
Mesquite	Strong earthy flavor.	Most meats, especially beef. Most vegetables.
Oak	The second most popular wood to use. Heavy smoke flavor. Red Oak is thought the best by pit masters.	Good with red meat, pork, fish and heavy game.
Pecan	Similar to hickory, but not as strong.	Good for most needs.
Cherry	The flavor is milder and sweeter than hickory.	Good on most meats.
Black Walnut	Very heavy smoke flavor, usually mixed with lighter wood like pecan or apple.	Good with red meats and game.

CPSIA information can be obtained
at www.ICGtesting.com
Printed in the USA
LVHW062018301220
675396LV00019B/1553

9 781649 840790